THE BIGGEST LIVING THING

Caroline Arnold

Carolrhoda Books • Minneapolis, Minnesota

With special thanks to the national park service
in Sequoia and Kings Canyon National Parks

Copyright © 1983 by CAROLRHODA BOOKS, INC.

Manufactured in the United States of America

LIBRARY OF CONGRESS CATALOGING IN PUBLICATION DATA

Arnold, Caroline
   The biggest living thing.

   (A Carolrhoda on my own book)
   Summary: Presents facts about the giant sequoia trees,
including how they grow, the circumstances of their
"discovery," how their age is determined, and how
forest fires actually help them.
   1. Giant sequoia—Juvenile literature. [1. Giant
sequoia. 2. Trees] I. Title. II. Series.
QK494.5.T3A76   1983   585'.2   83-1860
ISBN 0-87614-245-5   (lib. bdg.)

1 2 3 4 5 6 7 8 9 10 92 91 90 89 88 87 86 85 84 83

Giant Sequoia Trees

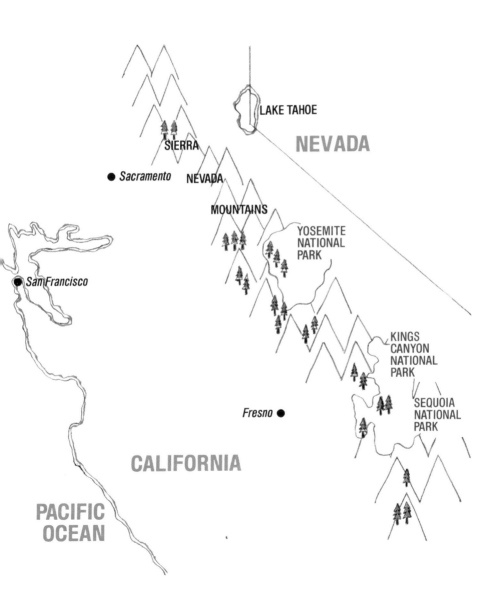

QUESTION: What plant

is taller than the Statue of Liberty?

weighs more than a big ship?

is bigger than any other living thing?

4

ANSWER:

A giant sequoia tree.
Giant sequoia (sih-KWOY-uh) trees
grow in the Sierra Nevada mountains
in California.
Most of the giant sequoias are in Sequoia,
Kings Canyon, and Yosemite national parks.
The biggest tree of all
grows in Sequoia National Park.
It is called the General Sherman Tree.
It is 272 feet tall,
and it weighs about 6,000 tons!

Some trees may grow taller
than giant sequoias.
Douglas fir, eucalyptus, and redwood trees
may be over 300 feet tall.

Redwood   Douglas Fir   Eucalyptus

But most trees are much smaller.
Oak and maple trees
are usually under 100 feet.
No tree, however, weighs more
than the giant sequoia.

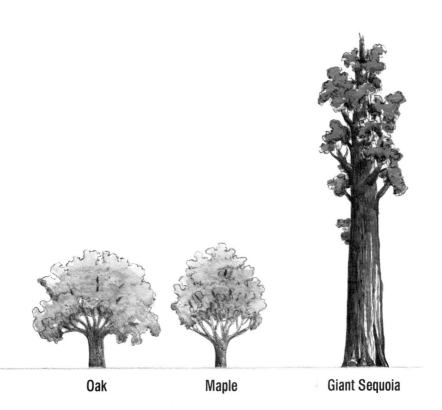

Oak   Maple   Giant Sequoia

The giant sequoia has a very thick trunk.
Sometimes a giant sequoia falls down.
Then people can weigh parts of it.
From this they can figure out
how much a living tree would weigh.

11

For a long time no one knew
about giant sequoia trees.
Then in 1848 gold was discovered
in California.
Men came from all over to look for gold.
They walked, they rode horses,
and they came in covered wagons.
They became gold miners.

The miners lived in camps
in the Sierra Nevada mountains.
One was called Murphy's Camp.
In 1852, a man named Augustus T. Dowd
worked at Murphy's Camp.
He was a hunter.
Each day he went into the forest
to hunt for food.
One day he made an amazing discovery.
He found a giant sequoia tree.
It grew high into the sky
and was bigger than anything
he had ever seen.
He didn't know it yet,
but it was the biggest tree in the world.

Dowd rushed back to camp.

He told everyone what he had seen.

They all laughed.

"You are fooling us!" they said.

"There is no such thing

as a tree that big."

No one believed him.

No one would go into the forest to look,

so Dowd decided to trick the miners.

He waited a few days.

Then he rushed back again from the forest.

This time he said, "Come quick!

I killed a big grizzly bear.

Help me bring it back!"

Everyone ran after him
to see the big grizzly bear.
Dowd led the miners
through the forest.
"Where is the bear?" they asked.
"We will see it soon," he said.
Just then they saw the giant sequoia tree.
Everyone stopped, amazed.
"See," said Augustus Dowd.
"There is no bear,
but there really is a giant tree."

The big trees were named after
a famous Cherokee Indian named Sequoya.
The spelling was changed to "sequoia"
for the trees.
Sequoya is most famous
for inventing a Cherokee alphabet.
He never saw a giant tree,
but the giant trees of the Sierras
were named in his honor.

Soon many people were coming to see
the giant trees.
A newspaperman
wrote a story about them.
It wasn't long before the whole world
knew about the giant sequoias.

Lumberjacks came to cut them down.

Visitors came to look at them.

Scientists came to study them.

Everybody wanted to know more
about the giant sequoias.

How old were they?

How did they grow to be so big?

The stumps of the giant sequoias
were huge.   One was so big,
it was used for a dance floor.
Thirty-two people
could dance on it at once!

On each stump there were rings.

Each year a tree grows two rings—

a light ring in the spring

and a dark ring in the summer.

In years of good weather the rings are fat.

In years of bad weather the rings are thin.

The lumberjacks counted the rings

on each stump.

Then they knew how old the tree had been.

One tree had 3,200 pairs of rings.

It was 3,200 years old!

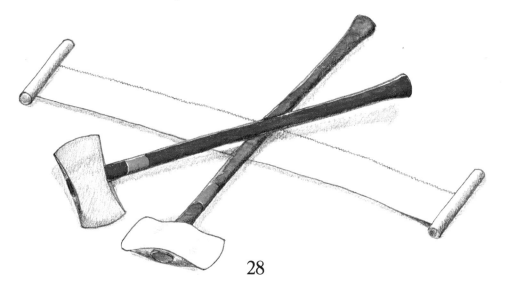

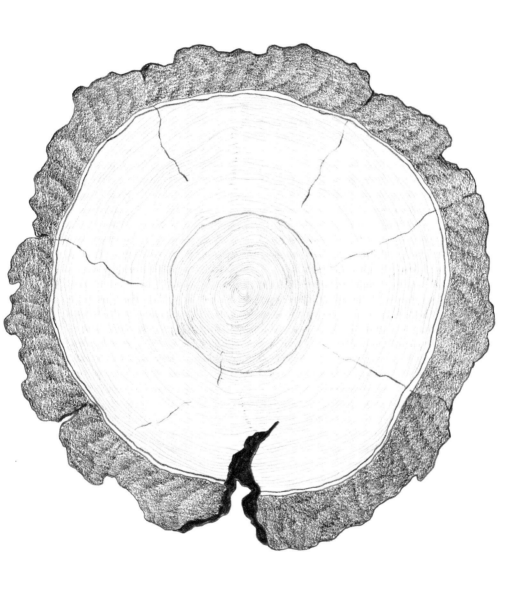

29

Each sequoia tree grows from a tiny seed.

The seed grows inside a pine cone.

When it is ripe, the seed falls to the earth.

The rain makes it damp.

The sun makes it warm.

Then it sprouts and grows.

First it grows into a tiny plant
called a seedling.
Each year the seedling gets bigger.
It will grow several inches a year
if it is not crowded
and if the weather is good.

2 week old
seedling

At first it looks like other pine trees.

When it is about 75 years old,

it may be over 100 feet tall.

Then the trunk becomes bare at the bottom.

The branches stick out like arms at the top.

The bark becomes dark red.

It begins to look like a giant sequoia.

5 years   25 years   75 years

1,000 years   2,000 years   3,000 years

The giant sequoia is like most plants.

It needs the sun, rain, and soil to grow.

But it needs one more thing too: fire!

Forest fire is a terrible thing,

but sometimes a small fire can be helpful.

Large giant sequoia trees

are not usually hurt by fire.

They have thick bark

that does not burn easily.

The bark protects the tree from fire.

A fire may leave scars,

but usually the tree is not burned down.

There are many ways in which
fire helps the giant sequoias.
Fire helps to prepare the ground
for the sequoia seeds.
They must fall on bare soil to grow.
Sometimes the ground is covered
with leaves and branches.
Then the seeds get lost
before they reach the soil.
Fire burns up this "garbage"
on the forest floor.

Fire also helps the seeds
come out of their cones.
Usually the seeds are held
tightly inside the cones.
Forest fires heat up the air.
This makes the cones dry out.
Then they open up.
The seeds fall down
onto the freshly prepared soil.
Seeds are also "planted"
by Douglas squirrels.
The squirrels like to eat
giant sequoia cones,
but they are messy eaters.
They drop some of the seeds.

Fires add minerals to the soil too.
Plants need minerals to grow,
and there are minerals in ashes.
Rain will soak these minerals
into the soil.

Fires also weed out the sequoia groves.

The fire kills other kinds of trees.

It also thins out small sequoia trees,

and it removes old and sick trees.

This gives the big trees room

to grow even bigger.

Once there was a tree

with a tunnel cut through its trunk.

It was so big,

you could drive a car right through it!

Then one winter night in 1969

the tunnel tree fell down.

Giant sequoia trees

usually do not get sick and die.

More often they fall over in big storms.

Sometimes their roots

are not strong enough to hold them up.

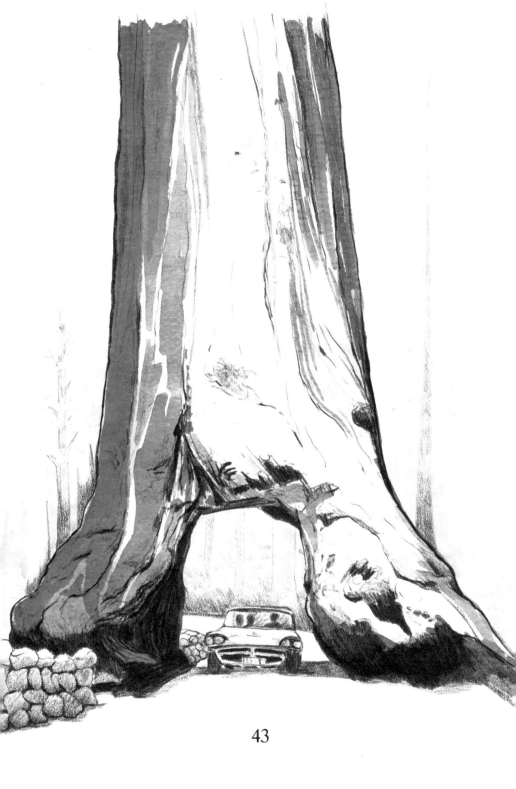

A man named Hale Tharp
once made his home
in the hollow trunk of a fallen tree.

The room inside that tree is 56 feet long.
It is eight feet tall at one end
and four feet tall at the other end!

Lumberjacks no longer
cut down the big trees.
Now the trees are protected
so that everyone can enjoy them.
Thousands of people visit
the sequoia trees every year.
The General Grant Tree in Grant's Grove
is our nation's Christmas tree.
Every year some people celebrate Christmas
under its branches.

The giant sequoia is a very special tree.
It is tall.
It is beautiful.
It is the biggest living thing.

About the Author

Caroline Arnold is well known for her many fine science books for young readers. Her *Animals that Migrate* was a New York Academy of Sciences Children's Book award winner as well as an NSTA-CBC Outstanding Science Trade Book for Children in 1982.

Ms. Arnold grew up in Minneapolis and studied art and literature at Grinnell College and the University of Iowa. She now lives in Los Angeles with her husband and two children. The Arnolds enjoy camping and have gone several times to the Sierras to camp and hike among the giant sequoias. It was on such a trip that Caroline Arnold first learned about the role of forest fire in the life cycle of the giant sequoia.